Somerset

Roger Evans

COUNTRYSIDE BOOKS
NEWBURY BERKSHIRE

First published 2008
© Roger Evans, 2008

COUNTRYSIDE BOOKS
3 Catherine Road
Newbury, Berkshire

To view our complete range of books,
please visit us at
www.countrysidebooks.co.uk

ISBN 978 1 84674 068 8

*Cover picture shows Compton Bishop
seen from Crook Peak*

Photographs by the author

Designed by Peter Davies, Nautilus Design
Maps by CJWT Solutions
Produced through MRM Associates Ltd, Reading
Typeset by CJWT Solutions, St Helens
Printed in Thailand

*All material for the manufacture of this book
was sourced from sustainable forests*

Contents

Area map showing location of the walks

POCKET PUB WALKS

Bridgwater Bay

Minehead
Shepton Mallet
Frome
Glastonbury
Bridgwater
Somerset
Taunton
Yeovil

Introduction

What finer way to spend your time than walking the Somerset countryside and rewarding the effort with good food and fine ales at a homely and welcoming pub. In this book I invite you to visit some of the many hostelries I have discovered on circular walks ranging from 2 to 6 miles. Fifteen choices are included, each with a pub on or very close to the route. Conveniently spread across the county, there should be one within easy reach for everyone – and others to discover not too far away.

Somerset is ideally suited to *Pocket Pub Walks*, with a fine selection of traditional pubs in such outstanding areas as the stone-walled high ground of Mendip and its isolated communities; the deep-cleft combes and valleys of West Somerset; the thatched cottages on Exmoor; and the rolling hills of South Somerset with its picturesque fawn-stone villages. The walks in this book capture that range of scenery and offer extra value to all who wish to experience the history and natural history of the county.

The featured pubs have been chosen for their warmth of reception, the quality of their food and ales, and many of them for their willingness to say 'Yes, dogs are always welcome'. Buster, my Border Collie, has been my constant companion throughout these walks and hence country pubs that welcome dogs are almost a prerequisite for me, as I know they are for so many walkers. The routes have also been carefully selected so as not to duplicate pubs and walks in my previous books (*Somerset Teashop Walks*, *Drive and Stroll in Somerset* and *Adventurous Pub Walks in Somerset*) and the reader can rest assured that each of these volumes adds to the list of walks available.

On all of these circuits I have used the appropriate Ordnance Survey Explorer map, and the required map number is given for each route. These will supplement the sketch maps and give you an overview of the surrounding area. The routes can take anything from an hour to three hours, according to how much time you take to 'stand and stare'. Remember, English weather can change rapidly, especially on the higher ground of the

Mendips and Exmoor, so I recommend wearing a sound pair of boots and appropriate clothing (ideally long trousers tucked into walking socks). Go well prepared, enjoy the scenery and savour the hospitality.

Happy walking!

Roger Evans

Publisher's Note

We hope that you obtain considerable enjoyment from this book; great care has been taken in its preparation. Although at the time of publication all routes followed public rights of way or permitted paths, diversion orders can be made and permissions withdrawn.

We cannot, of course, be held responsible for such diversion orders and any inaccuracies in the text which result from these or any other changes to the routes nor any damage which might result from walkers trespassing on private property. We are anxious though that all details covering the walks are kept up to date and would therefore welcome information from readers which would be relevant to future editions.

The simple sketch maps that accompany the walks in this book are based on notes made by the author whilst checking out the routes on the ground. They are designed to show you how to reach the start, to point out the main features of the overall circuit, and they contain a progression of numbers that relate to the paragraphs of the text.

However, for the benefit of a proper map, we do recommend that you purchase the relevant Ordnance Survey sheet covering your walk. The Ordnance Survey maps are widely available, especially through booksellers and local newsagents.

1 Porlock

The Royal Oak

Porlock shelters beneath the slopes of Exmoor and is perfectly positioned for walking and touring in the area. At one time, it was a coastal town but the recession of the sea has left it well inland, with nearby Porlock Weir now serving as the local harbour. The shops provide for the needs of both tourism and the farming community. Along the roads, which are extremely narrow in places, there are colourful cottages and the local inns would once have been frequented by the many poets who favoured the area.

Somerset

Distance – 4 miles.

OS Explorer OL9 Exmoor. GR 885467.
Uphill at the start but thereafter more level. Well-defined tracks with no stiles through mostly woodland walking.

Starting point Porlock central car park – pay and display.

How to get there Porlock is easy to find on the main A39 to the west of Minehead. The car park is well signposted just to the north of the High Street by following the road to Porlock Weir for a few yards and then turning right.

The Royal Oak, featured here, had its literary links, and the nearby Ship Inn, an old coaching house, was enjoyed by Coleridge and Wordsworth; it was also where their friend Robert Southey penned the lines: 'Porlock, I shall forget thee not, Here by the unwelcome summer rain confined.' Furthermore it is the inn where R.D. Blackmore placed the highwayman Tom Faggus.

After an initial steepish climb, this is a most pleasant walk following Hawk Combe as it rises up onto Exmoor through some of the most ancient woodland in the country. Dippers, buzzards, pied flycatchers are all possibilities and, of course, the red deer, which are numerous on most parts of the moor.

THE PUB The **Royal Oak**, which can easily be found in the High Street, not far from the car park in Porlock's High Street, is a friendly pub dating back to 1724. It was the favoured haunt of R.D. Blackmore, author of *Lorna Doone*. Once closed down for rowdiness, it was allowed to reopen in 1880 and is now a welcoming place selling real ales including Wells Bombardier, Courage Best and a guest ale. Home-made food, which is really good, is featured on a specials board. Well-behaved dogs are very welcome and are sometimes greeted with a dog chew as a treat.

Open daily from 11 am (12 noon on Sundays) to 11 pm (11.30 pm on Fridays). Meals are served from 12.30 pm to 2.30 pm and 6.30 pm to 9.30 pm throughout the week.
☎ *01643 862798*

1 Leave the car park by following the signs to the public library and then turn left onto the main road. Just before the village church, turn right into **Parson Street**.

2 At the public toilets, turn right onto a bridleway signposted for **Hawkcombe**. Continue uphill until another path comes uphill to join yours. Keep on uphill as the path zigzags towards the ridge, turning right after passing through a metal gate. The path is joined by a low wall along one side, with a welcome bench set back into it.

3 On reaching the end of the low wall, the path splits. Walk to the left, continuing uphill into a sunken track. At **Halsecombe**

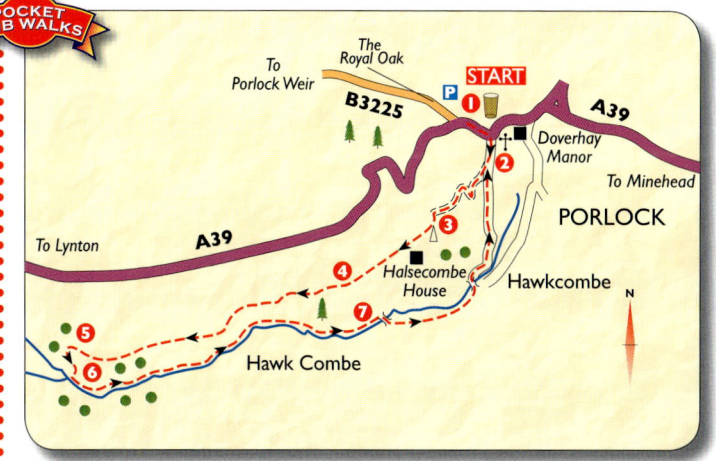

A watermill in Hawk Combe.

House, which is up on the ridge, continue straight ahead to enter a field via a blue waymarked gate. Keep to the left-hand field boundary to reach a pair of gates.

4 Take the gate on the left, which leads you into the woodland. Follow the bridleway ahead; there are occasional blue waymarkers. The bridleway becomes a terraced track hugging the right-hand edge of the woodland for about a mile until reaching a track at a crossroads.

5 Turn left to head downhill for about 150 yards and then turn left onto a terraced track This gradually drops down to a wider track where you turn right to head downhill to the stream, which runs down to **Porlock**.

6 Turn left to follow the wide track downstream, eventually reaching a group of houses where the track becomes a tarred lane running down through the woods.

7 Turn right at a high wall onto a signposted footpath to cross a footbridge. Climb gradually uphill for about 200 yards to meet another track, which is marked with a 'No Horses' sign. Turn left here to descend slowly down to a road and parking area. Turn left over the stream and then right into **Mill Lane**, which takes you back down to **Parson Street** and the **High Street**.

Places of interest nearby

Porlock Weir is a very pleasant spot to spend an evening after a day's walk, with its row of fishermen's cottages and small craft bobbing in the harbour. It is also a good starting point for a short stroll (about a mile each way) to **Culbone church**, the smallest parish church in England. No road goes there and it is at that isolated spot that Samuel Taylor Coleridge sat down to write *Kubla Khan*, until a man from Porlock interrupted his thoughts! Church services are still held here but not every week.

Close to the church in Porlock, the 15th-century **Doverhay Manor** now serves as a tourist information centre and a museum, with a small collection of artefacts, paintings and photos. There is also a pleasant herb garden maintained by a team of volunteers. Visitors may be interested to discover the story of how the Lynmouth lifeboat was hauled over Countisbury Hill and down into Porlock on a storm-swept night in a sea-rescue that is now legend.

☎ *Manor/museum 01643 862645*
☎ *Tourist information centre 01643 863150*

The George Inn

Brompton Regis, formerly known as King's Brompton, lies at the southern foot of the Brendon Hills, about 5 miles north of Dulverton. This walk crosses fields from the village to reach the shores of Wimbleball Lake, a majestic stretch of water in the Exmoor National Park, surrounded by woodland and meadows. A huge man-made reservoir, this serves the needs of the city of Exeter and provides excellent opportunities for water sports and fishing. Completed in 1979, it impounds water from the River Haddeo and has a surface area of 374 acres, providing one of Exmoor's finest assets.

Distance – 5½ miles.

OS Explorer OL9 Exmoor. GR 951315.
Relatively easy walking, moderate ascents, fields, footpaths and lakeside. Some footbridges and stiles.

Starting point The free parking area by the village hall. An alternative start point is at Wimbleball Lake (pay and display parking) at point 4, which allows a visit to the George Inn before completing the return trip.

How to get there If approaching from the west or south, take the A396 between Tiverton and Dunster; head east, signposted to Brompton Regis. Knightstone Mead, your parking area, will be on your right as you enter the village. From the east, on the B3224, just west of Raleigh's Cross, turn left onto the B3190; turn right, signposted to Brompton Regis. On the far side of the village centre, turn left into Knightstone Mead just after the village hall.

After a pleasant walk southwards along the lake shore, the route crosses the dam, providing splendid views, before turning onto Lady Harriet's Drive, a pleasant track through ancient oak woodland. Lady Harriet was the wife of Major Acland who fought for the British in the American War of Independence. He was wounded and taken prisoner. Lady Harriet, hearing the news, crossed the Hudson River to nurse her husband. No wonder he named a drive after that very special lady! The return trip then follows woodlands and lanes back to the village.

THE PUB Located in the centre of Brompton Regis, the **George Inn** is a traditional and friendly 16th-century hostelry. It is a free house with good quality home-made meals from local produce available each day of the week. Well-kept real ales from the Exmoor brewery are served plus guest beers. Well-behaved dogs are welcome.

For those seeking an overnight stay, there is en-suite accommodation with a private barn cottage next door available for self-caterers. In the entrance hall, the visitor will find plenty of information on local activities such as sailing and canoeing on the nearby Wimbleball Lake, cycling, riding and, of course, walking. With the Brendon Hills all around, the George offers a great central point for a few days of activity.

Open daily from 12 noon to 2.30 pm and 7 pm to 11 pm (Sundays 10.30 pm). Lunches from 12 noon to 2 pm and evening meals 7 pm to 9 pm.
☎ 01396 371273; email: thegeorgeexmoor@btconnect.com

1 Leave the car park by turning right, going past the village hall. After the **George Inn**, turn right through an iron gate into a narrow lane, which runs downhill past the church to reach a lane. Turn right onto the lane, going past the post office.

2 Just before the speed limit signs, turn left onto a footpath heading downhill to a stream. Cross the footbridge and follow the track as its bears right and then left before reaching a T-junction. Turn right and continue to a metalled road. Turn right at the road to reach a house on the left-hand side in about 200 yards.

3 Just before the house, turn left onto a footpath signposted 'Wimbleball'. Cross two stiles to enter a field and then, bearing right, follow the right-hand field boundary downhill to cross the stream over a footbridge. Go through a gate to enter the next field and then follow the right-hand field boundaries across a number of fields, maintaining the same line of direction, to reach a metalled road. Turn right and then go left into the main entrance of the **Wimbleball Lake Water Park**. Keep straight ahead, past the play area, to reach the lake shore.

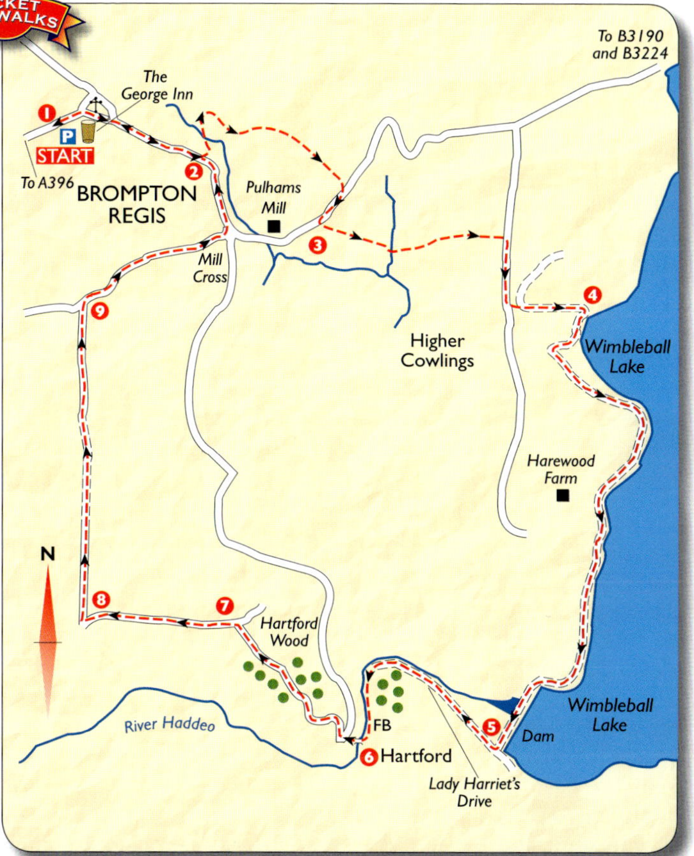

To B3190
and B3224

The
George Inn

1
P
START

To A396   **BROMPTON
REGIS**

2

Pulhams
Mill

Mill
Cross

3

Higher
Cowlings

4

*Wimbleball
Lake*

Harewood
Farm

9

N

8   **7**

*Hartford
Wood*

River Haddeo

FB

6 Hartford   **5**   Dam

*Lady Harriet's
Drive*

*Wimbleball
Lake*

4 Turn right and follow the path as it turns around the back of
the sailing club, signposted as 'Lakeside walk, dam ¾ mile'.
Follow the obvious path past **Harewood Farm** to your right
and cross a wooden bridge over a dyke, eventually to enter
Eastern Wood. Emerging from the wood, bear right to reach
and cross the dam.

Yachts line the shore at Wimbleball Lake.

5 Once across the dam, turn right, signposted '**Bury 2½ miles**' to go down a metalled road. By ignoring any side routes you travel along **Lady Harriet's Drive**. At the bottom of the track, after passing through a gate, as you approach a bridge, bear left onto a green track signposted '**Bridleway to Bury**' to reach a ford. Cross the footbridge, signposted as a footpath, and then bear left to follow the river on the other side.

6 Just after passing a house, turn right through a gate (**Hartford Mill**) to reach a track with several signs at a small triangular junction. Turn right at this junction of tracks onto a path which is not signposted but in just a few yards you will find an uphill path to the left signposted as '**Louisa Gate, Dulverton and Brompton Regis**' to follow a zigzag track to the hilltop.

In about 400 yards, the path splits. Take the right-hand track to reach a crossroads of tracks with a green track in front of you. Turn left and in about 10 yards at a fork, turn right and continue uphill to a crossroads where you continue straight ahead, keeping uphill, and likewise at the next crossroads, maintaining your uphill ascent to reach the top edge of the woodland. (NB: the OS map shows a confusion of forestry tracks in this area. If in doubt, just head north-west and uphill to reach the ridge where the required track will be found at the woodland edge.)

7 Turn left here with the woodland on your left and a high tree-lined bank on your right, with fields on the other side.

8 In about 500 yards, turn right to enter a tree-lined path heading north. Be careful not to miss this break in the embankment. Continue straight ahead along tracks following left-hand field boundaries, over a number of stiles, until you reach a metalled road.

9 Turn right down to the crossroads at **Mill Cross** where you turn left to head back into Brompton Regis.

Place of interest nearby

Wimbleball Lake is the nearest significant attraction and is well worth a visit beyond that which this walk provides. With canoeing, sailing, wind surfing and trout fishing from shore or boat, there are plenty of activities in a stunning location. Beginners and experts are catered for and hire facilities are available; the centre is open from Easter to the end of October. Organised events include a rowing regatta in June, the 'Exmoor Beastie' sailing event in March, guided walks and even a two-day country fair in May. There is pay and display parking.
☎ 01398 371460

For those who seek a longer, more adventurous walk, what could be simpler than to complete the around-the-lake 9-mile walk, finishing up at the tea rooms and perhaps retiring to the nearby campsite.

The Luttrell Arms

Dunster village, which can be very busy with summer traffic, has a magnificent centre with its craft and teashops clustered around the medieval octagonal yarn market. Beyond can be seen the splendid Dunster Castle. The early part of the walk is steeply uphill along Conduit Lane down which once ran the village water supply from St Leonard's Well, which is passed on the route. The return journey is along Grabbist Hill and it was here in 1848 that Cecil F. Alexander composed the children's hymn *All things bright and beautiful* – and it's easy to see why with such outstanding views across the hills to the Somerset coast.

Parts of the **Luttrell Arms** date back to 1443 when it served as a guesthouse for the abbots of Cleeve. Today it provides a perfect centre from which to explore the Exmoor National Park. It has a restaurant with an impressive à la carte menu of modern and classic dishes plus two bars where bar snacks are provided. The beers on offer include Exmoor Fox from the local Exmoor Ales brewery, Wadworth's 6X and a weekly guest beer. The open log fires make it a most enjoyable place to visit in the winter months, and in the summer the gardens provide an alfresco alternative. Accommodation is available, including rooms with four-poster beds. Well-behaved dogs are welcome.

Open daily from 11 am to 11 pm. Meal times, including bar snacks, are from 11.30 am to 2.30 pm and 7 pm to 9 pm (10 pm during the summer season).
☎ *01643 821555*
Website: www.luttrellarms.co.uk

Distance – 4½ miles.

OS Explorer OL9 Exmoor. GR 992438.
Some steep climbs, particularly at the start, are rewarded with fine views. The return journey is fairly level most of the way and then descends swiftly to Dunster village. Forests and open moorland.

Starting point The main car park at Dunster.

How to get there *Leave the A39 about a mile west of Minehead and take the A396 signposted for Dunster. In a few hundred yards, turn left into the large pay and display car park. There are toilet facilities at the top of this car park.*

Somerset

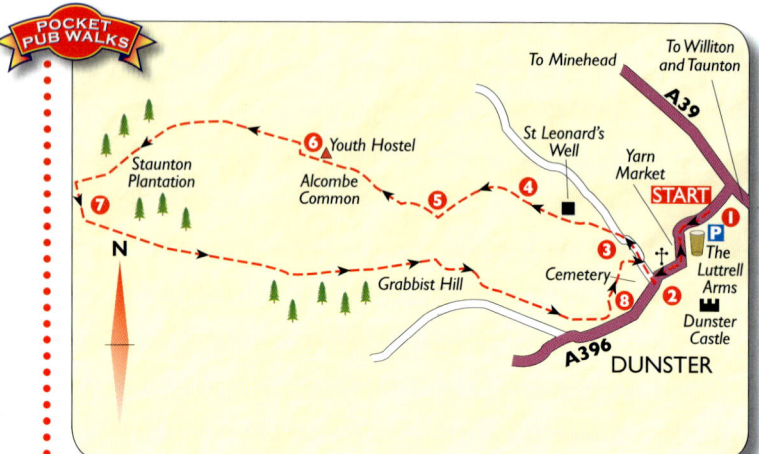

1 Leave the car park from the top end and follow the village road uphill past the **Tourist Information Office**. Take care along the next stretch, which has no pavement on either side. Continue uphill, bearing left around a corner with the **Luttrell Arms** on your left-hand side. This brings you into Dunster's **High Street** with its distinctive **yarn market** in the middle of the road and views to the **castle** immediately ahead. Continue along the **High Street**, bearing right, past the traffic lights, into **Church Street**.

2 Turn right into **St George's Street** going past **Priory Green**, which can be seen through an arch on your right. Continue uphill until you reach a double turning on your left, one heading south, almost doubling back to the left, and the other heading west.

3 Take this latter track heading up **Conduit Lane**, a green track, which leads up to **St Leonard's Well**. On reaching the well, you meet woodland, and a track leads off to the left destined for **Grabbist Hill**. Ignore that path and continue straight ahead.

4 The route now begins to level off, with the worst of the uphill climb behind you. Continue to the next fork where you take the left-hand path as it curves around the hillside along the left-hand side of the woodland.

5 You come to a junction of many tracks. Turn right here, signposted for **Alcombe**. Continue ahead for about ½ mile, passing to the left of the youth hostel on **Alcombe Common**.

6 Just after the track takes a sharp left turn, you join a road where you turn right and in a few yards come to a triangular junction. Turn left to cross a stream and enter **Staunton Plantation**. Continue straight ahead along the main track climbing constantly up through the combe until a turn to the left takes you out of the plantation. At the next junction turn left, signposted to **Dunster**.

7 There is now a wide and obvious track to follow, which takes you along the ridge of **Grabbist Hill**. Ignore the various paths off to

Dunster's medieval yarn market with the castle in the background.

each side, following the main track until eventually it starts its descent down towards the village. Then take the right-hand path towards **Dunster Castle**.

8 In ⅓ mile, go through a gate, passing to the left of a cemetery. On reaching a second cemetery, after passing allotments, turn right through the gate into the cemetery, following the line of trees to reach a road. Turn right into **St George's Street** and, retracing your earlier steps, head down into the centre of the village to find the **Luttrell Arms** and around the corner from the inn continue down to your car park.

Places of interest nearby

There is much to see in Dunster. The most obvious attraction is **Dunster Castle** on its dramatic hilltop location where it dominates the village. Now in the ownership of the National Trust, it has a romantic atmosphere with its turrets and towers. The castle has had a turbulent past. A thousand years ago, at which time the sea came right up to the foot of the castle, it defended our shores from Viking invaders, and likewise from the invasion of the Celts. Today the scene is a peaceful one with its sub-tropical terraced gardens, which include the national collection of strawberry trees.

☎ 01643 821314

Also worth a visit, particularly for those with children, is the **Dunster Doll Museum** in the Dunster Memorial Hall. It holds a unique collection of over 800 dolls from historic to modern and includes a magnificent doll's house and many christening gowns. Open from Easter to September 10.30 am to 4.30 pm on weekdays and 2 pm to 5 pm at weekends.

4 **Wiveliscombe**

The Bear Inn

Wiveliscombe, or Wivvy as it is known locally, is a small town set in beautiful countryside. It is just a few miles from the Devon border at the foot of the Brendon Hills and as such acts as one of the gateways to Exmoor. Despite its small population, its shops serve the needs of a much larger rural community scattered around the hills of this corner of the county, and it is perhaps best known as a brewing centre with two local breweries. It is an ideal centre for cycling and especially walking, being located on the West Deane Way, a recently opened long-distance footpath.

This circuit takes the walker through that scenery, mostly along tracks and quiet country lanes, and over a few fields, following the higher reaches of the River Tone for a good stretch midway along the walk.

THE PUB

The **Bear Inn**, which can be found in North Street by turning left as you leave the car park, is full of character. As a former 17th-century coaching inn, there isn't a straight wall or level floor to be found in the place and hence it has masses of old world ambience. It is even claimed that upstairs the floor is so uneven that it compensates for the effect of one too many! The pub, which serves real ales from the town's two breweries, Exmoor and Cotleigh, has a warm and friendly atmosphere. The food is good quality and home-cooked. Inside you will find an open fire on cold days, and outside there is a large beer garden and play area. Dogs are welcome both in the pub and on the patio. Overnight accommodation is available. There is a car park for the use of patrons – just ensure that the landlord knows if you are going to leave your car there for any length of time.

Open daily from 11 am (midday on Sunday) to 11 pm (midnight on Thursday, Friday and Saturday). Food is served from 12 noon to 2.30 pm and 6 pm to 9 pm.
☎ *01984 623537*

Distance – 6 miles.

OS Explorer 128 Taunton & Blackdown Hills. GR 080280. Mostly fields and woodland with pleasant stretches of riverside walking along the West Deane Way. Some steep ascents in the middle section.

Starting point The free car park in North Street, Wiveliscombe.

How to get there *Wiveliscombe will be found 8 miles west of Taunton on the B3227. In the centre of the town, at a crossroads, turn north into the High Street, continue ahead into North Street and the car park is on your right.*

1 Leave the car park by turning left into **North Street**, passing the **Bear Inn** on your way, to continue down into the **High Street**. At the traffic lights, turn left and in a short distance turn right to go down steps and under an arch into **Rotton Row**. Head straight down this, turning left into **South Street**. Continue towards the edge of the town and shortly after **Southfield** (on your right), turn right into a lane.

2 Where the lane bears right, go straight ahead through a gate, following a footpath sign. Continue straight ahead to cross a stile and follow the left-hand field boundary for two fields, keeping in the same direction, to reach another stile. This may be overgrown, in which case walk on for about 25 yards to reach a gate and go through this.

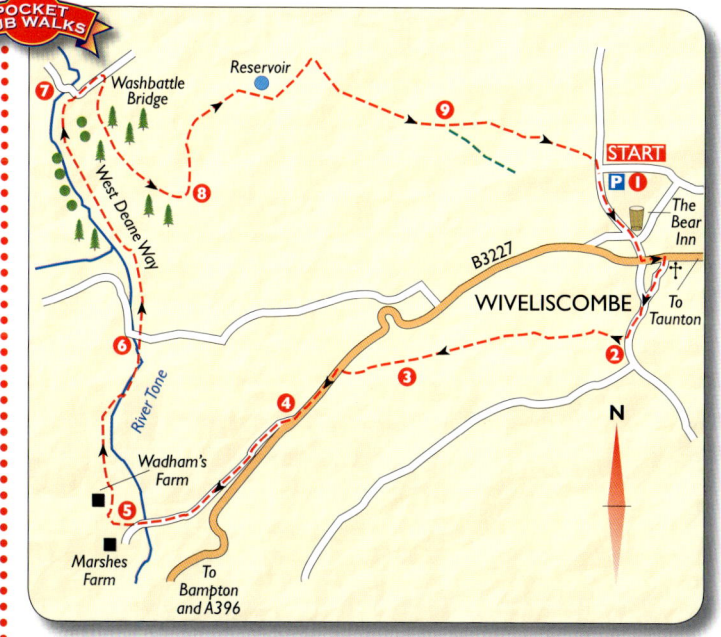

3 Continue in the same direction as before to reach a group of farm buildings. Beyond these, keep in the same previous direction, following the left-hand field boundary up to the metalled road. Turn left.

4 Where the road forks, turn right to head fairly steeply downhill to cross the **River Tone**. Continue straight ahead, uphill, to where the road bears left at **Marshes**

The ornate public library at Wiveliscombe.

Farm. Keep straight ahead here (not following the road as it bears left) onto a signposted bridleway. Avoid the right turn into the farm but continue ahead, going steeply uphill to reach a sunken lane between high banks.

5 Turn right into the sunken lane heading towards **Wadham's Farm**, turning left just as you reach the first farm building on a track which follows the river. This is the **West Deane Way**, a recent addition to long-distance walking routes. Continue along this track until reaching a T-junction as you approach a group of houses. Turn right at the junction to cross a footbridge and then go left to emerge onto the metalled road, **Challick Lane**.

6 Cross the road to continue along the **West Deane Way**, following the **River Tone** upstream until reaching another metalled road at **Washbattle Bridge**.

7 Turn right onto the road. In about 200 yards, turn right onto a signposted forestry road and head uphill to reach the top where you bear left onto a wide track, continuing uphill. On emerging from the woods into a field, bear right to reach the right-hand field boundary, which you follow uphill to reach a gate.

8 Go through the gate and turn left to pass through another gate onto a track lined with hedgerows. Follow this track as it curves around to the right, passing a reservoir at the head of the hill. The track bears left and then straightens up before reaching a metalled road, which leads to the left. Turn sharp right here to follow a track, which descends back towards **Wiveliscombe**.

9 In about ½ mile, where the lane forks, turn left onto a track which becomes a metalled road leading back down into the town, where your car park and the **Bear Inn** will be found.

Places of interest nearby

For lovers of truly fine gardens, **Cothay Manor** at Greenham, 4 miles to the south of Wiveliscombe, is well worth a visit. Built in 1480, it has remained virtually untouched as a classic medieval manor house, perhaps the most perfect in the country, with its Great Hall, Oratory and Great Chamber. It is decorated with unique wall paintings and sits in 12 acres of wonderful gardens along the River Tone. It's the gardens that make this place special and have earned it the maximum two stars in the *Good Garden Guide*. Open Easter to the end of September on Wednesday, Thursday and Sunday afternoons.
☎ 01823 672283

The Bicknoller Inn

Bicknoller is one of the many picturesque villages scattered around the lower slopes of the Quantock Hills. It was this area of Somerset that provided much of the inspiration for the poets Samuel Taylor Coleridge and William and Dorothy Wordsworth, all three living nearby during their most productive period. This is red deer country and almost a thousand of these fine animals occupy the Quantock Hills providing good opportunities to view them in the wild, especially for those prepared to travel quietly. During the October rutting season, the stags can be heard as they bellow to attract the females. Hunting goes on throughout the year, deer on Mondays and Thursdays, foxes on Tuesdays and Saturdays.

The route for this walk is short and sweet, travelling up a combe to reach the moorland edge, then gently following the contours before descending down through another combe and across a few fields back into the village of Bicknoller.

THE PUB The **Bicknoller Inn** is a 14th-century village pub that was once a coaching stop. With thatched roof, stone floors and wooden beams, it retains much of that old character and in colder weather a real log fire is cosy and welcoming. The food is excellent and the restaurant offers an impressive range of meals based on local produce, which means that the menus are changing daily. Everything from bar snacks of sandwiches and bangers and mash to full three-course dinners are available. In fact, there can be few pubs that offer such an extensive range of food. Check their website for details – see below. Booking is advised, especially for Sunday lunch. Real ales from Palmer's and cider from Thatcher's are on draught. Children and well-behaved dogs are welcome and there is a beer garden.

Distance – 2 miles.

OS Explorer 140 Quantock Hills & Bridgwater. GR 109392. Easy underfoot with short inclines. Some track and field walking. If accompanied by a dog, be prepared for 'frisky horses' in point 4.

Starting point The Bicknoller Inn car park (for use of patrons). There is also ample roadside parking around the village.

How to get there *From the A358 between Taunton and Williton, turn north-east into Church Lane, signposted for Bicknoller, and the Bicknoller Inn will easily be found near the centre of the village.*

Opening times are 11 am to 11 pm daily during the summer months and on Friday, Saturday and Sunday throughout the year. In the winter months, 11 am to 3 pm and 6 pm to 11 pm on Monday to Thursday. Meals are served from midday to 2.30 pm and 6 pm to 9 pm.

☎ *01984 656234; website: www.bicknollerinn.co.uk*

1 From the **Bicknoller Inn**, head uphill along **Church Lane**, past the church on your right, to reach a T-junction with **Trendle Lane**. Turn left. Ignore the left turn into **Dashwood Lane** and continue for a few yards.

2 Turn right at a crossroads, by the post office, into a lane marked as a no through road. This is **Hill Lane** and you are now joining the **Macmillan Way West** as you head up into **Bicknoller**

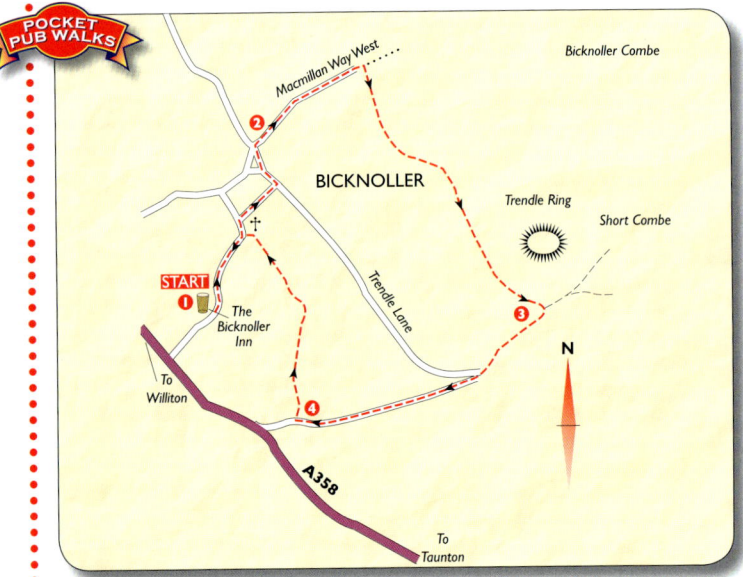

Straight from the horse's mouth: 'Frisky Horses'.

Combe, heading towards **Bicknoller Hill**. Continue up this track to its end, passing through a farm gate into National Trust property. Turn immediately right at the NT notice onto a track signposted '**Quantock Moor**'. This leads more steeply uphill with fields to your right and open moorland to your left. The track soon levels out and you will be following the right-hand edge of the moor. Follow this path for ½ mile, with the **Trendle Ring Iron Age site** to your left and wonderful views across to the **Brendon Hills** to your right as you pass through a small wooden gate. You soon cross a small stream where you reach a cluster of houses at '**Short Combe**', which comes down from your left.

3 Turn right here to head downhill along a tarmac and gravel road. In about 200 yards, you reach a junction of tracks at **Trendle Lane** (you could turn right here to head back into the village, if you wish, avoiding the fields where frisky horses reside). Go straight ahead into **Chilcombe Lane**. Continue for just over ½ mile. As the road in front begins to bear left, a thatched cottage will be on your left.

4 Just before the cottage, turn right into a field through a six-bar metal gate with a half-hidden yellow marker. Keeping the cottage grounds to your left, head straight across the field to cross an easily spotted stile and stream into the next field. Go over two more fields in like fashion, keeping the church tower diagonally to your left, crossing the easily spotted stiles as you go. In the final and much larger field, head towards the church tower to reach the village road where you turn left for the **Bicknoller Inn**.

Cautionary note for dog walkers: each time I have walked these last two fields, they have contained a group of horses. A notice warning of 'Frisky Horses' is only seen as you leave. These horses are quite friendly to people but have chased my Border Collie relentlessly.

Places of interest nearby

Combe Sydenham Country Park will be found just 3 miles south-west of Bicknoller and nestles in a hidden valley at the village of Monksilver. The old manor house, which dates back to 1580, was built in the E-shaped fashion for Sir George Sydenham, and was rebuilt in 1660 after the Restoration. Reminders of Sir George's daughter's marriage to Sir Francis Drake are kept here, and tales of the most unusual events leading to that marriage and of the local dragon plus the Duke of Wellington could be the reward for a visit to the house. The manor is set on a 500-acre estate with a large herd of fallow deer and beautiful woodland that provides plenty of walks. There is even a downhill bike course. The country park is open from April to September, 9 am to 5 pm. Guided tours of the West Wing, gardens and corn mill are available from May to September on Mondays, Wednesdays and Thursdays at 1.30 pm.
☎ 01984 656284

POCKET PUB WALKS

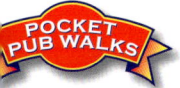

6 Nether Stowey

The Ancient Mariner

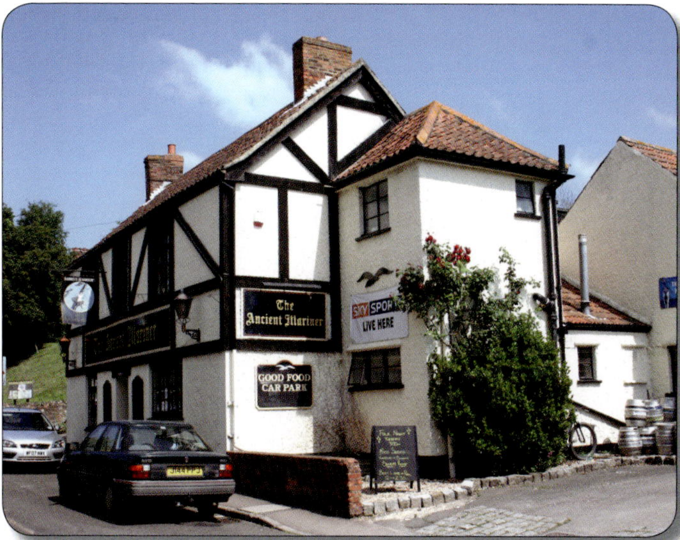

Nether Stowey is a delightful village which was once the home of Samuel Taylor Coleridge. Thomas Poole, a local tanner, encouraged Coleridge to stay here and his former home is now in the ownership of the National Trust. Coleridge, in turn, brought William and Dorothy Wordsworth to nearby Holford, and it was during their time in these Quantock villages that they walked the hills and found the inspiration for their finest poetry. This walk retraces their steps up into the wooded combes, full of rich birdsong through the spring and summer

Distance – 5 miles.

OS Explorer 140 Quantock Hills & Bridgwater. GR 191397. Mostly very quiet lanes, tracks and woodland walking (which can be sticky after rain). Some climbs on the outward leg but nothing too strenuous.

Starting point Free car park at the Nether Stowey library and Quantock Hills AONB offices. (There is also parking for patrons at the Ancient Mariner in Lime Street.)

How to get there *Nether Stowey is well signposted from the A39 between Bridgwater and Minehead. On reaching the village centre, turn uphill into Castle Street. The car park is a short distance up the hill on the right-hand side. The Ancient Mariner will be found close to the village centre in Lime Street, opposite Coleridge Cottage.*

months. It takes you past the site of Walford's Gibbet where John Walford was hanged for murdering his wife. It sounds gruesome but the views are exceptional, as they are from the site of Stowey Castle, an 11th-century motte and bailey defensive position which is passed along the route.

THE PUB The **Ancient Mariner** was once a 17th-century coaching inn, before the days of the village bypass, housing its own blacksmith. The friendly atmosphere identified with such old establishments survives today and the welcome is a genuine one. It's a warm and friendly free house, normally with four real ales on tap, serving steaks, fish, seafood and the more traditional pub fare. Tuesday nights are fun with folk sessions alternating with quizzes. There is a large beer garden and a patio with a spacious play area for children. Well-behaved dogs are welcome.

Opening hours: Monday 6 pm to 11 pm; Tuesday to Friday 12 noon to 3 pm and 6 pm to 11 pm; weekends 12 noon to midnight (11 pm on Sunday). Meals are served from midday to 2.30 pm and 6 pm to 8.30 pm.
☎ *01278 733544*

1 On leaving the car park, turn right to head uphill and take the third turning right into **Butcher's Lane**, marked as unsuitable for motor vehicles. Continue to the T-junction. Turn left, heading uphill, and in about 200 yards turn right into **Hack Lane**. Continue for ½ mile.

2 Turn left onto a track running between two hedgerows with mature trees on the right-hand side. In about 400 yards, the track swings to the left.

3 At this point, keep to the same line of direction by crossing a stile on your right-hand side into a field. Follow the left-hand field boundary. Keep straight ahead along this line, reaching

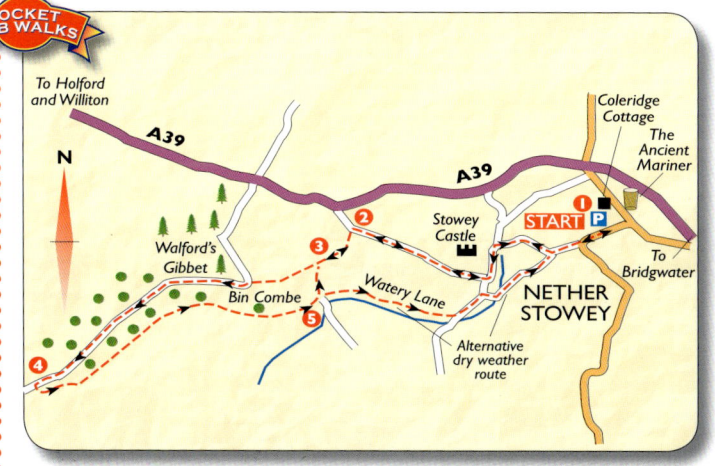

Red deer stags on the Quantocks. (Courtesy of Diane Trout)

a disused quarry on your left. The hedge-line kinks to the left around the quarry, at which point you need to head half-right to the top of the field to reach a gate and a metalled road. This is the old coach road. Turn left and head gently uphill through a wooded combe with the valley on your left-hand side. In ¾ mile, the road dips slightly before resuming its uphill journey. Just as it begins to climb, trees stand along a low overgrown wall.

4 Just after the wall there is a waymarked track to the left but this is not your track. Take the unmarked track to the left immediately before the wall and continue down to the bed of the combe.

5 Eventually you reach a crossroad of tracks. It is possible to go straight ahead into **Watery Lane** and back to the village, but as its name suggests, this route can be very sticky and is best left for dry days. The alternative is to turn left at the crossroads and follow the track back to point 3, from where you can retrace your steps back to the village enjoying the expansive views across the Bristol Channel.

Places of interest nearby

Coleridge Cottage will be found at 35 Lime Street in Nether Stowey, immediately opposite the Ancient Mariner. Samuel Taylor Coleridge lived here from 1797 for three years and many of his mementoes are on display. It was here that he wrote the finest of his works including *The Rime of the Ancient Mariner, Frost at Midnight, Kubla Khan* and *Christabel*. He became close friends with William and Dorothy Wordsworth, whom he persuaded to move into Alfoxden House at Holford. They spent many hours walking the hills together, finding mutual inspiration through the relationship. The cottage was constructed in the 17th century as a simple building with a parlour, kitchen and service room. Upstairs were three very small bedrooms. The kitchen was so small that Sara, Coleridge's wife, struggled to use it successfully. At the rear is the long garden, which reaches down to meet the bottom end of the garden of Thomas Poole, Coleridge's sponsor. It was in Poole's garden that Coleridge wrote *This Lime Tree Bower* when confined there after Sara had managed to scald his foot by dropping a skillet of milk. The house is open from 2 pm to 5 pm on Thursdays to Sundays and Bank Holiday Mondays from April to September.
☎ 01278 732662

The Ruishton Inn

This is a nice, easy walk along level riverside and canalside paths. Before the days of motorways and A-roads, all movement of heavy goods was along the rivers, and the River Tone was the traders' route into the county town of Taunton. However, problems with tides and occasional low waters necessitated the introduction of a canal from Taunton to Bridgwater, with the two running almost side-by-side along this walk. The canal was started at Taunton in 1820 when it reached as far as Huntworth, and then the link to Bridgwater was completed in 1841. The canal towpath now forms part of the Sustrans national cycle network, route number 3.

THE PUB The **Ruishton Inn**, dating back to 1861 and known locally as the 'Rui', is a Wadworth-owned village pub serving traditional beers straight from the wood. These include Henry's IPA, 6X and Bishop's Tipple, my personal favourite.

Distance – 3¾ miles.

OS Explorer 128 Taunton & Blackdown Hills. GR 264251. Flat and easy waterside walking. Some stiles. Very easy to follow route. This is a nice safe walk where dogs can be off the lead if under control. However, the short section of A38 (in point 2) is very busy and dogs need to be on a lead there. The safest place to cross is at the traffic lights mentioned below.

Starting point Ruishton Inn car park (parking available for patrons).

How to get there *From junction 25 of the M5 motorway, take the A358 towards Ilminster and in 100 yards turn left into Ruishton Lane. In 600 yards, the Ruishton Inn will be found on the left-hand side at the junction of Church Lane and Cleats Lane. Patrons can use the pub car park with the consent of the landlord. Otherwise Church Lane offers some kerbside parking.*

This is a comfortable, friendly place and generous portions of good quality home-cooked food are on offer. The wide-ranging menu includes seasonal specials using local produce. But if you're in a hurry, they even offer curries and fish and chips as take-aways. Children and dogs are welcome and the beer garden is popular in the summer months.

Opening times: midday to 2.30 pm daily (except Mondays) and 6 pm to 11.30 pm (7 pm to 11 pm on Sundays). Meals are served from midday to 2 pm and 6 pm to 9 pm (7 pm to 9 pm on Sundays). A traditional Sunday lunch is served but bookings are essential.
☎ *01823 442285*

1 Leave the pub car park by turning right and immediately right again into **Church Lane**. At the church, take the lane to its left and follow this over a footbridge, keeping straight ahead to reach the bank of the **River Tone**. Turn left and keep to the top of the riverbank, going under the motorway bridge. Continue until you come to a lake.

2 Take the right-hand path at the lake, up to the **Hankridge** interpretation panel, and cross a footbridge, keeping the river to your right. Continue along the riverside path, ignoring the footbridge to the right, which crosses the river, until reaching a stile onto the A38 at **Bathpool**. Turn right, passing over the river and then the railway, and continue past **Yew Tree Lane** to reach a set of traffic lights. Cross the road at the lights and turn right to maintain your previous direction. Take the second turning on the left into **Swingbridge** and then bear right to reach a canal swing bridge in about 200 yards.

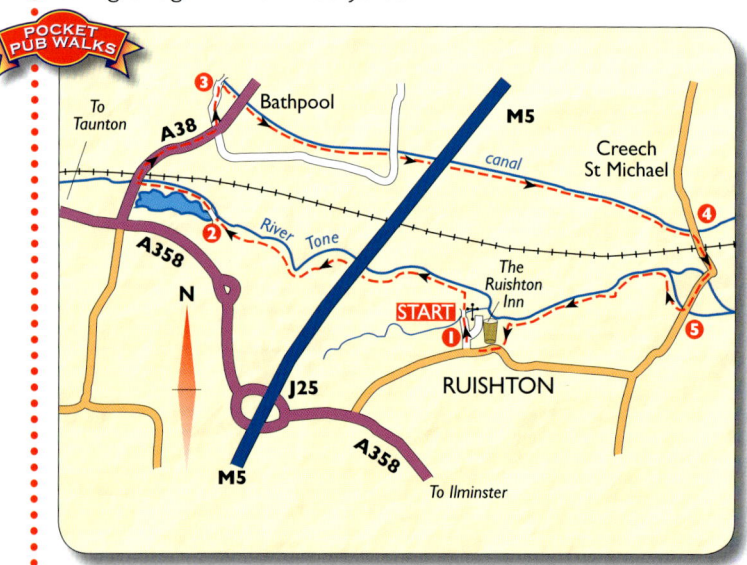

The swing bridge at Bathpool (point 3 on the route).

3 Just before the bridge, turn right onto the canalside towpath. Follow this to go back under the motorway and in about the same distance again you will reach the B-road at **Creech St Michael**.

4 Pass under the bridge and then turn right up onto the road. Turn left and follow the road, crossing the bridge over the railway lines. In about 100 yards, the road bears right and then crosses the **River Tone** twice.

5 Immediately after the second crossing, with **Ham Road** on your left, turn right to cross a stile into a field and follow the riverside footpath all the way back to **Ruishton** where the path ends at a stile at the back of a row of bungalows. Cross the stile into **Goosey Lane**, at the end of which you turn right to return to the **Ruishton Inn**.

Places of interest nearby

The **Willows and Wetlands visitor centre**, 5 miles east of Ruishton at Meare Green Court in Stoke St Gregory, was opened by David Bellamy in 1987, endorsing its green credentials. In warm weather it abounds with a wide range of butterflies and warblers. The centre is owned by the Coate family who have been growing willows here since 1819. Visitors can learn about the history of willow growing and the art of basket making. Naturally there is a fine selection of basketware available for purchase all of which has been handcrafted by skilled basket makers. The range goes from purely decorative to the totally practical, including indoor and outdoor furniture, and DIY kits are available for those who wish to test their skills.

Admission is free and includes a video room, a museum of willow artefacts and an interpretation centre that tells how the Somerset Levels have been shaped. As a working factory, access to the workshop is only in escorted groups. A leaflet detailing unguided walks can be picked up in the shop and gives a choice of an easy and flat walk through the willow beds or a longer walk along the Tone and up to a viewpoint at Windmill Hill.

The centre is open on Monday to Saturday from 9 am to 5 pm. There are guided tours on Monday to Friday from 10 am to midday and 2 pm to 4 pm but not on bank holidays.

☎ 01823 490249.

8 Cross and Crook Peak

The White Hart

The distinctive summit of Crook Peak catches my eye and beckons another ascent whenever I travel north on the M5. Travelling south it is this landmark that says I'm not far from home. It's one of those distinctive high points that deserve to be visited and it rewards the walker with stunning views. By including Wavering Down, this route takes in two peaks, giving double value for the effort. This western end of the Mendip

Distance – 5 miles.

OS Explorer 153 Weston-super-Mare & Bleadon Hill. GR 415547.
Most of the route is on open moorland, with some riverside walking. The early part of the circuit is steeply uphill but brings its reward with fine views. There is a steep-in-places descent mid-walk as you come down from Crook Peak and this is best done in dry weather.

Starting point The White Hart's car park at Cross (for patrons) by kind consent of the licensees. Ample roadside parking as an alternative can be found between points 6 and 1 on the route where long lay-bys exist.

How to get there *From the A38, 4 miles south of Churchill, turn west onto the Cross road. In about 400 yards you pass the New Inn and the White Hart will be found a short distance further on.*

Hills is limestone country and in spring and summer provides a richness of flora and insect life. Lizards and adders also abound, the latter being perfectly safe when left alone. The grazing by roe deer and rabbits provides comfortable walking underfoot.

THE PUB
The **White Hart** is a 17th-century former coaching house on the old highway from Bristol to Bridgwater and, naturally, it can boast the resident ghost of a rebel who fell victim to the Bloody Assizes after the 1685 Monmouth Rebellion. These days there is a warm and friendly welcome with a good choice of food from bar snacks to a full three-course meal. The real ales include Courage, Butcombe's and Black Sheep. Dogs are welcome and the children can even meet Daisy, the friendly pig that lives in the back paddock.

Cross and Crook Peak Walk 8

Opening times: daily from midday to 11 pm (11.30 pm on Thursdays, midnight on Fridays and Saturdays). Meals are served Tuesday evenings to Sunday lunchtimes from midday to 2 pm and 6 pm to 9 pm.
☎ 01934 732260

1 Leave the pub car park and head west. Pass a turning on your left, the continuation of the **Old Coach Road**, and turn right into **Bourton Lane**.

2 At **Bourton Farm**, turn left before the farmhouse to go past a whitewashed cottage and through a metal gate. Turn right once through the gate to head uphill, following the right-hand field boundary. On reaching two gates, take the one on the left and

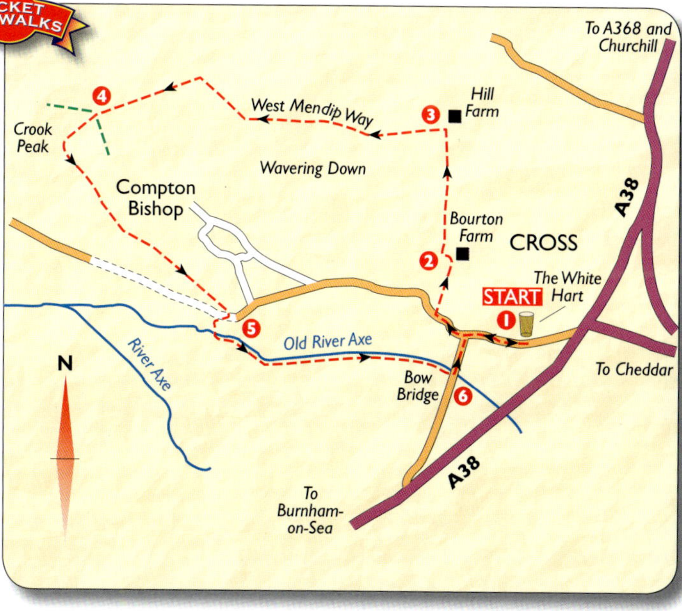

POCKET PUB WALKS

Map showing the walk route with the following labels:

To A368 and Churchill

Hill Farm **3**

4

West Mendip Way

Crook Peak

Wavering Down

Compton Bishop

Bourton Farm **2**

CROSS

A38

The White Hart

START **1**

Old River Axe

5

River Axe

Bow Bridge **6**

To Cheddar

N

A38

To Burnham-on-Sea

The M5 sweeps its way below the heights of Crook Peak.

continue in the same uphill direction, ignoring any diversions on the way, to reach the ridge track at **Hill Farm**, which stands at the right-hand end of a line of trees.

3 Turn left to follow the well-defined **West Mendip Way**, following the right-hand field boundary with a stone wall on your right to reach and pass the triangulation point. Continue following the wall as it kinks right and then left, eventually reaching its end as it turns off to the right.

4 At the end of the wall, follow the obvious path up to the distinctive **Crook Peak**. At the peak, bear left to take the well-trodden path that heads in a south-easterly direction down the ridge above the southern slope from Crook Peak, with the village of **Compton Bishop** to your left and the **River Axe** to your right. Ignore any side turnings by just keeping to the same line of direction as you pass the top of a quarry (caution – long drop!) and eventually reach the village road.

5 Look for the lane opposite, which bears right past some buildings. Take this lane and in a matter of a few yards, turn left through a metal gate onto a footpath signed as a private road. Follow this path to cross the **Old River Axe**, where you turn left over a stile and then follow the river, keeping it on your left, for a mile until you reach the **Old Coach Road** at **Bow Bridge**.

6 Turn left and then right at the T-junction, with **Webbington Road** to your left, to return to the **White Hart**.

Places of interest nearby

Just 3 miles east of Cross is the town of **Cheddar** with its world famous caves and gorge. This has been a major tourist attraction for over 200 years, and it's easy to see why, with the cathedral-like caves including the magnificent Diamond Chamber and Solomon's Temple, carved out a million years ago. The underground complex was discovered by George Cox in 1837 when one of his workmen fell through a hole in the roof of a cave while he was collecting stone for building materials. They were re-discovered in 1890 by Richard Gough. An Explorer ticket allows you to benefit from a number of attractions including the caves, a walk up Jacob's Ladder to a high-placed look-out tower and an open-top bus ride (in season) up through the gorge itself. ☎ 01934 742343; website: www.visitcheddar.co.uk

9 Hinton St George

The Lord Poulett Arms

The villages of South Somerset have a character of their own, quintessentially English with thatched roofs and walls built from the local Ham Hill stone, golden-fawn in colour which softens in the evening sunlight to provide a warm and comfortable feeling. Hinton St George is one of the best of such villages and is well blessed with the Poulett Arms as the local pub. This is dairy country close to the Dorset border, and the walk passes along quiet lanes and through enclosed fields along footpaths and bridleways. A short section of the circuit is along the old Fosse Way used by the Romans to link Exeter to Lincoln in as close to a straight line as they could achieve. The final section of the walk, as you rise from a valley bed, provides wonderful views across the south Somerset landscape.

Distance – 3 miles.

OS Explorer 129 Yeovil & Sherborne. GR 421126.
Fairly level walking along quiet lanes and footpaths through farmland. Several stiles and some stretches can be sticky but passable after heavy rain. Gentle gradients on the return route.

Starting point The Lord Poulett Arms in the High Street. There is ample opportunity for safe roadside parking in the area.

How to get there *At the A303 South Petherton roundabout, take the B-road south-west, signposted for Lopen. As you pass out of the other side of Lopen village, turn right, signposted for Hinton St George. At the village centre crossroads, turn right into the High Street. The Poulett Arms will be on your right-hand side.*

THE PUB

The **Lord Poulett Arms** at Hinton St George is a carefully restored 17th-century inn set in one of Somerset's prettiest villages. It offers some of the best food in this part of the county in a 'real fire' setting. This is not a 'pie and a pint' pub. The food, including a wide range of meats and fish, is taken seriously. Outside there is a walled herb garden where customers can play boules and where an ancient fives court survives. For those wishing to dine alfresco, there is the shade of a pergola, or you can take your meal under an apple tree in the wild meadow.

Opening times: midday to 3 pm and 6.30 pm to 11 pm daily. Meals are served from midday to 2 pm and 7 pm to 9 pm.
☎ *01460 73149*

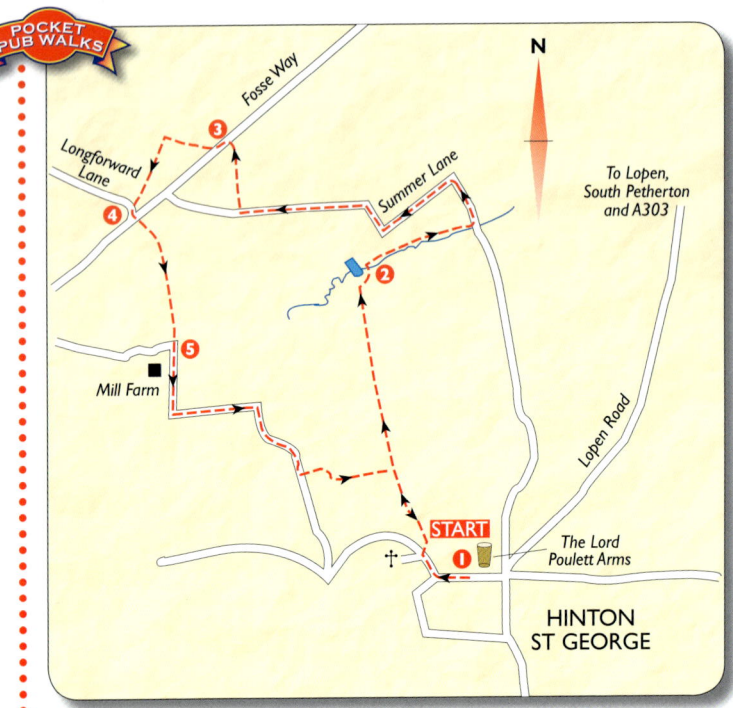

POCKET PUB WALKS

Fosse Way

Longforward Lane

Summer Lane

❸

❹

❷

❺

Mill Farm

To Lopen,
South Petherton
and A303

Lopen Road

N

START

The Lord
Poulett Arms

HINTON
ST GEORGE

1 From the **Lord Poulett Arms**, turn right to head west along the **High Street**, aiming for the raised market cross at the road junction. Pass to the right of the cross following the road as it bears right. Just opposite the lane to the church, turn right onto a footpath signposted to 'Lopen 1½ m; Crimbleford Knap 1¼ m'. Ignore the gate to your right and follow the path as it bears left and drops down to a kissing gate. Pass through the gate and follow the signed footpath straight ahead, following the right-hand field boundary. Cross the stile into the next field and keep to the same line of direction but this time following the left-hand field boundary, and likewise into the next field, switching back to the right-hand field boundary.

The colourful main road through Hinton St George.

2 Cross the next stile and then a small bridge to reach a pond. Turn right at the pond and follow it partway around and then turn right to follow the stream you have just crossed, keeping the stream on your right-hand side until you reach the metalled road, **Summer Lane**, at a stile. Turn left onto the metalled road, following the lane as it kinks to the left, right and left again as it tracks a large field on your right. At the end of the field, a footpath sign indicates the route to the Fosse Way. Take that footpath by entering the field and following the right-hand field boundary to reach the metalled road at the **Fosse Way**.

3 Turn left onto the road and in 50 yards turn right into another field to follow the footpath, heading slightly left of straight ahead to reach the far field boundary where you turn left, keeping the field boundary to your right until you reach a metalled road once again.

4 Turn left onto **Longforward Lane** to return to the **Fosse Way**. Go straight across onto a footpath signposted to **Hinton St George**, following the right-hand field boundary until you reach a gate where the field boundary bears left. Go through the gate and go straight ahead, dropping down through the field to cross a stream and pass through two gates onto the lane at **Mill Farm**.

5 Go straight ahead onto the lane, following it as it turns left, then right, then swings left and bears right again. In about 50 yards, as you start to climb towards the ridge in front of you, turn left onto a track signposted to **Hinton St George**. Follow this until you reach the track that was the first section of your outward journey. Turn right to retrace your route back to the **Lord Poulett Arms**.

Places of interest nearby

   Montacute House, about 6 miles from Hinton St George, just off the A3088 west of Yeovil, is one of the finest properties in the ownership of the National Trust and has often been used for film locations such as the 1995 *Sense and Sensibility*. This stone-built Renaissance manor house is packed full of treasures including a collection of 17th-century textile samplers, reflecting south Somerset's textile-based past, and Elizabethan artwork housed in the Long Gallery, believed to be the longest such gallery in the country. The gardens are deservedly famous and contain two pudding houses, so called because in Elizabethan times, the family would leave the dining room and head for these small garden houses to take their puddings. Most of the 300 acres of grounds are available for the public to explore. It is best to check the opening times before visiting.
☎ 01935 823289

10 **Rodney Stoke**

The Rodney Stoke Inn

This is a pleasant walk along the southern slopes of the Mendip Hills; it is in the heart of the local strawberry-growing territory and even vineyards can be seen along the route. The circuit starts almost down on the Somerset Levels and ascends to one of the highest points on the Mendips. This section of the route is an old drovers' track once used to move sheep and cattle between high and low ground according to the seasons. Naturally the views are stunning, especially on clear days so, although the initial ascent is quite steep, it pays to stop frequently to take in the ever-changing scenery. At the highest point of the walk, the well-defined West Mendip Way is joined. In fact the whole route is well defined, making navigation quite

Distance – 3 miles

OS Explorer 141 Cheddar Gorge & Mendip Hills West. GR 484502.
Steep ascent at the start. A few easy stiles and clear paths all the way. The climb is rewarded with fine views. Easy underfoot at most times of the year.

Starting point The Rodney Stoke Inn. Patrons may use the car park; otherwise roadside parking can be difficult, the roads being narrow in the area around the pub but opportunities relatively close to the pub can be found.

How to get there On the A371 between Cheddar and Wells, 3 miles from Cheddar. The Rodney Stoke Inn is on Wells Road in the centre of the village at the junction with Butts Lane.

easy. The final stretch is fairly level walking through pleasant meadowland as you wend your way back to the Rodney Stoke Inn.

THE PUB

The **Rodney Stoke Inn** is well placed on the sunny south face of the Mendip Hills where it has served the needs of travellers for centuries past. It was rebuilt in 1914 with real stone walls and an open fireplace. Internally, as well as the bar, there is a larger area for dining, with patio windows. A real little gem, it serves good quality hot and cold meals at lunchtimes and in the evenings, with a daily specials board supporting the standard pub grub. The menu caters for children, and colouring sheets and crayons are provided for the youngsters. Local beers include Butcombe's, brewed nearby on the Mendips. Outside is a beer garden and patio with well-tended flowerbeds and hanging baskets – a most pleasant setting. Well-behaved dogs are welcome in the garden.

Opening times: daily 11 am to 11 pm. Meals are served from 12 noon to 2.30 pm and 6.30 pm to 9.30 pm. Telephone: 01749 870209

1 Take the tarmac lane (**Hill Lane**) immediately opposite the **Rodney Stoke Inn**, which is marked as a no through road. Follow this to its end where it becomes a gravel track and continue uphill between the stone walls on either side.

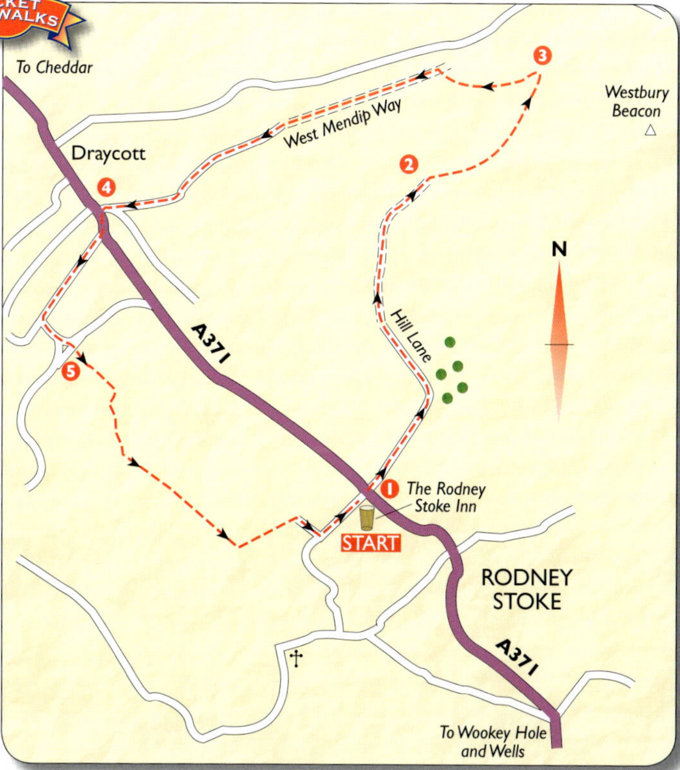

POCKET PUB WALKS

To Cheddar

West Mendip Way

Westbury Beacon

Draycott

3

2

4

N

A371

Hill Lane

5

1 The Rodney Stoke Inn

START

RODNEY STOKE

A371

To Wookey Hole and Wells

Rodney Stoke is at the heart of this strawberry-growing area.

2 At the end of the stone walls, which mark the end of the drovers' track, go through the gate and continue straight ahead towards a derelict hut, passing to the right of the hut. After the hut bear slightly left, heading towards the ridge and the left-hand end of a line of trees growing on top of a stone wall.

3 Reaching the tree-lined wall, you will have joined the **West Mendip Way**.

*To your right is the high ground of **Westbury Beacon**. It is worth a short detour to admire the excellent views which on a clear day can extend to 50 miles. Cross the stile, heading for the high point, cross another stile and then make your way to the top before retracing your steps.*

Turn left onto the **West Mendip Way**, going over a stile to follow a walled hedge-line along the frequently stiled and well-signposted path down into the village of **Draycott**.

4 On reaching the A371 at the village war memorial, turn left and then right into **Wet Lane**. Continue down the lane until it meets a road at a junction, where you turn left and then immediately left again where the road forks.

5 At the next road, go straight across into the dead-end **Eastville Lane**, passing through a housing estate, and then across meadowland, heading for the clearly seen **Rodney Stoke church**. In about 400 yards, it appears that the path is about to enter the grounds of a private house. Pass to the right of the house through a wooden stile. In another 400 yards, turn left onto a tarmac path, then after the lane bears right, turn left to reach the A371 at the junction where you will find the **Rodney Stoke Inn**.

Places of interest nearby

Wookey Hole Caves, on the outskirts of Wells, are a major tourist attraction in Somerset and are reached via the A371 to the south-east of Rodney Stoke. The caves were formed by the action of the River Axe. As the waters leave the cave system, which is open to the public, they flow alongside the paper mill that is part of the complex. The caves are most particularly noted for the Witch of Wookey, a human-shaped rock. Allegedly the witch was turned to stone by a local monk. The caves stay at a constant temperature of 11°C, ideal for the storage of the local Cheddar cheese. But there's much more at this attraction, especially for children, with the 'Valley of Dinosaurs', the 'Enchanted Fairy Garden, a puppet show and the 'Magical Mirror Maze'. Opening times: April to October, 10 am to 5 pm; November to March 10 am to 4 pm. Closed Christmas Day.

The Castlebrook Inn

Compton Dundon lies at the eastern end of the Polden Hills, the smallest of the Somerset ranges. This finger-like ridge almost points from Glastonbury to the sea, cutting across the Somerset Levels between the peat moors below Mendip and the alluvial clay moors below the Blackdown and Quantock Hills. Both of these low moors were once under the sea and Polden villages like Compton Dundon were seaside dwelling places. Here and there, large islands stood out in the sea, which we now recognise as Glastonbury Tor, Brent Knoll and Dundon Hill, around which this walk skirts. As you progress along the walk, which takes in quiet lanes and footpaths, picture how it once would have looked when all the low-lying fields were below sea level, indeed some of them still are under water on occasions.

Distance – 4 miles.

OS Explorer 141 Cheddar Gorge & Mendip Hills West.
GR 491326.
Fairly level with some moderate slopes. Nothing strenuous,
mostly lanes and tracks.

Starting point The Castlebrook Inn car park (for the use of
patrons). Otherwise, on-road parking is limited along this
fast stretch of road, and a more practical alternative is to
start at point 3 on the route, where a left turn from Hayes
Lane into Moor Close provides spacious layby parking.

How to get there *The inn is easily found in the centre of
the village on the main B3151 road between Street and
Somerton.*

THE PUB The **Castlebrook Inn** at Compton Dundon is a traditional
village pub dating back to 1540 and was once a coaching
inn. It has an inglenook fireplace and offers a friendly
welcome and cosy atmosphere. The restaurant was a medieval
hall and dates back to the 12th century. Good home-cooked
food is served all day and there is a carvery on Sunday. The beer
garden is particularly large, extending to over an acre. Children
and dogs are welcome.

*Opening hours: midday to 11 pm (although they describe it
as 'open until we shut!'). Meals are served throughout the day
from midday to 9.15 pm. Telephone: 01458 443632*

1 From the **Castlebrook Inn** car park, turn left and head south on
the B3151 to find a waymarked footpath entrance into the fields
on your right-hand side. Follow the right-hand field boundary

to reach a stile on the far side of the field. Cross the stile (which you will also cross on your return journey) and turn left. Follow the left-hand field boundary for five fields to emerge onto a metalled road.

2 Turn right and continue along the road as it bears right around the lower edge of **Dundon Hill** which will be on your right-hand side.

3 In the village of **Dundon**, turn left into **Hayes Lane**. Ignore a turning to your left and go straight ahead into a no through road (ignore the footpath on the right to **Lollover Hill**). Continue for ½ mile.

4 When the lane bears left where phone lines cross, turn right onto a wide hedge-lined track. Continue ahead, ignoring a waymarked stile on your left, and follow the lane as it turns right and heads uphill back to the village road at a T-junction in **Dundon**.

5 Turn left and, with the church ahead of you, bear right to follow the road. In a few yards, fork right into a no through road with

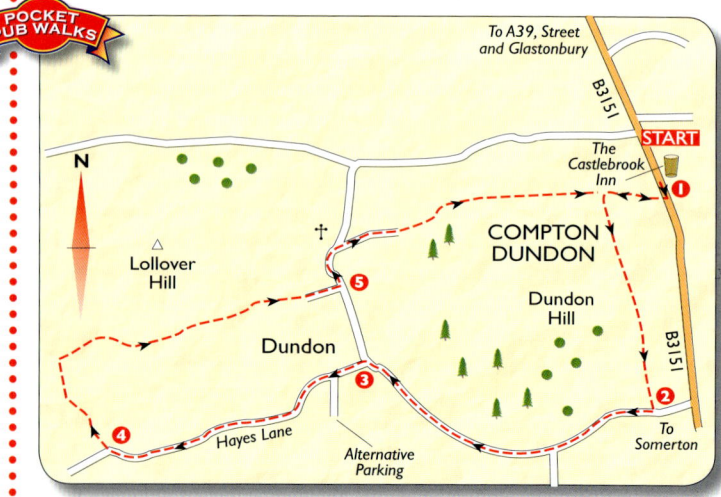

a school on your right. Continue along this hedge-lined track, ignoring the signed footpath on your right. Follow the track as it curves right with the woodland to your right. Ignore the footpath that peels off to your left and simply follow the left-hand field boundaries for three fields to reach the stile you crossed in the first section of the walk. Retrace your steps to the **Castlebrook Inn**.

Dundon Hill in the background, approaching point 5.

Places of interest nearby

The **Somerset Rural Life Museum** at Glastonbury is an excellent place to visit, especially for families. In the Abbey Farmhouse, the rooms have been reconstructed to depict Victorian life in Somerset and an exhibition tells the story of the life of farm worker John Hodge. The Abbey Barn, a magnificent 14th-century building, is at the very heart of the museum and contains a wealth of agricultural memorabilia. Further displays are exhibited in the various buildings that surround a courtyard, beyond which sheep and chickens run freely in the orchard. Willow growing, mud-horse fishing, peat digging and cider making are among the rural activities covered. To add to the temptation, there is ample free parking around the back of the museum and admission is free. Opening times: April to October, Tuesday to Friday and Bank Holiday Mondays, 10 am to 5 pm, weekends 2 pm to 6 pm; November to March, Tuesday to Saturday, 10 am to 5 pm; closed on Good Friday.
☎ 01458 831197

12 East Coker

The Helyar Arms

South Somerset is ideal for walkers, especially those who seek an alternative to the hilly terrains of Exmoor and the Mendips. East Coker is typical of many villages in the area, having ancient and pretty thatched houses built with the warm-looking Ham Hill stone, their walls bedecked with rambling roses, wisteria and honeysuckle in summer. In one of these homes once lived the former pirate William Dampier who explored the west coast of Australia and was the navigator on the ship that rescued Alexander Selkirk, the marooned sailor who inspired the novel of *Robinson Crusoe*. East Coker is also the birthplace of the poet T.S. Eliot. His ashes rest in the local churchyard. The walk skirts the grounds of Grade II Coker Court with its 15th-century hall and 18th-century wings, the one-time home of the Helyar family after whom the village pub takes its name.

Distance – 3½ miles.

OS Explorer 129 Yeovil & Sherborne. GR 537128.
An easy walk on quiet lanes and footpaths. Gentle slopes with extensive views and picturesque village settings.

Starting point The village hall car park in East Coker. There is also ample parking for patrons at the nearby Helyar Arms (see map).

How to get there *From Yeovil, take the A30 West Coker road and turn left at the post office into Sandhurst Road, signposted for East Coker. At the T-junction in North Coker, turn left and then take the next turning right to find the village hall car park. Alternatively, instead of turning right, go straight on to the Helyar Arms, which will be on your left-hand side.*

THE PUB

The **Helyar Arms** in Moor Lane, East Coker has won a whole host of awards. Dating back to 1468, it oozes with character. The main bar area, warmed in the winter by a log fire, retains many of the Elizabethan features with its beamed ceilings and is packed with old furniture, horse brasses and jugs. The usual range of bar snacks is available and the old apple loft is used as a dining area where a wide selection of offerings is on the menu. The quality is of a very high standard and produce is sourced locally – take a look at the website for details. Outside there is a garden area.

Opening times: 11 am to 3 pm and 6 pm to 11 pm on Monday to Friday; Saturday 11 am to 11 pm; Sunday 12 noon to 10.30 pm. Meals are served from midday to 2.30 pm and 6.30 pm to 9.30 pm.
☎ *01935 862332; website: www.helyar-arms.co.uk*

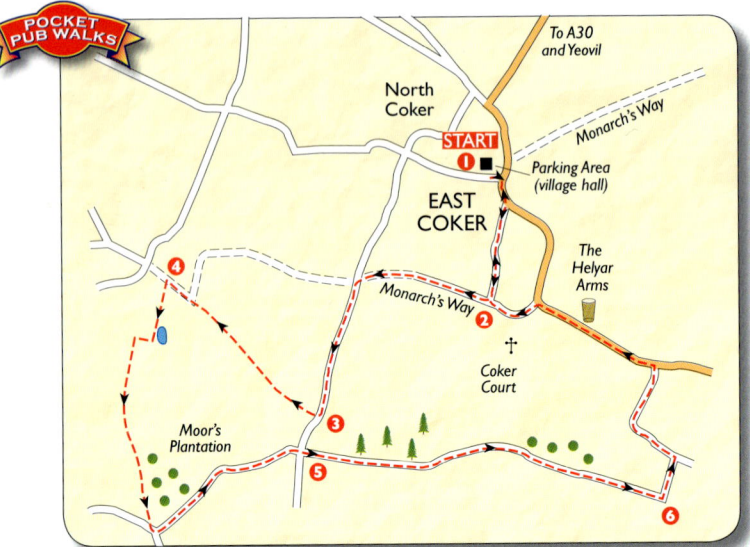

1 Leave the village hall car park by turning left and at the T-junction turn right towards the centre of **East Coker**. In 50 yards, take the hedge-lined footpath to the right up over a small hill to reach a T-junction with **Back Lane**.

2 Turn right. You are now on the long-distance **Monarch's Way** footpath. Pass through a kissing gate onto a tree-lined avenue and after going through another kissing gate you reach a metalled road. Turn left at the road and head up and over the ridge of the low hill in front for ¼ mile.

3 Just over the brow, where a tennis court is on your left-hand side, turn right to cross a stile. Keep straight ahead alongside the right-hand field boundary, following the contours of the hillside with views over the **Hardington Valley** on your left. Cross two fields and stiles in this direction until the track becomes a lane at a large house.

East Coker Walk 12

4 In 40 yards, just after **Merry Moles**, turn left to cross a stile. Go straight ahead, following the right-hand field boundary, to go past a lake, Cross the stile into the next field and continue slightly to the right of straight ahead to reach a gap in the hedge at the lower end of the field. Cross into the next field and go straight ahead, uphill, to reach the far field boundary just to the right of **Moor's Plantation**. Cross into the next field and, keeping the plantation on your left, go straight ahead to reach the metalled road. Turn left onto the road and follow this for ½ mile to a crossroads by a bungalow.

5 Go straight over at the crossroads into a no through road. Follow this for nearly a mile, with **Coker Court** to your left.

6 Turn left onto **Stoney Lane**, heading downhill to a T-junction. Turn left again and follow the lane, around the right-hand bend, to reach the village road. Turn left onto the road and in 400 yards you will reach the **Helyar Arms**. About 100 yards past the pub, where the road bears right, turn left and in another 100 yards, turn right to retrace your steps to the car park.

Places of interest nearby

The **Fleet Air Arm Museum** at Yeovilton is one of the largest aircraft museums in the world with over 90 planes on display. Exhibits cover World Wars I and II, the Falklands conflict, the Korean War, the Women's Royal Naval Service and much more, all concerning the history of naval aviation. Opening times: April to October, daily from 10 am to 5.30 pm (last admission 4 pm); November to March, Wednesday to Sunday, 10 am to 4.30 pm (last admission 4 p.m.); closed Christmas Day and Boxing Day. The museum is located near Ilchester on the B3151 just off the A303 and A37.
☎ 01935 840565

The Fountain Inn

W**here else can you walk** from a city centre to the open countryside in under five minutes? Wells is England's smallest city and is blessed with perhaps the finest cathedral in the country. This is an ideal route for those long summer evenings when the low-setting sun provides a warm glow to the magnificent west face of the cathedral. The circuit takes in this fine aspect and continues along the moat of the Bishop's Palace where you can spot the small bell placed outside of a window just over the moat. The short rope that hangs down is tugged by the swans when they wish to summon lunch. Following the cathedral grounds, the route of this walk crosses fields on well-made footpaths and then heads modestly uphill, through woodland, before turning back along well-defined paths to the city centre.

Distance – 2 miles

OS Explorer 141 Cheddar Gorge & Mendip Hills West. GR 552460.
Generally easy underfoot. One steep but brief ascent. A short woodland section can be sticky after wet weather. Some stiles but otherwise easy walking.

Starting point Fountain Inn car park, 1 St Thomas Street, Wells. Parking is limited in the pub car park and is for patrons only. An alternative is to use the long-stay pay and display car park in Chamberlain Street, which is well signposted.

How to get there *From the A39 relief road, follow signs for 'Hotels and deliveries' into New Street. Turn left at the roundabout, signposted 'The Horringtons', into The Liberty. Continue to a pedestrian crossing where the pub car park is on your right and the pub on your left. From the Shepton Mallet A371 road, head for the city centre to the end of Tor Street where the pub is directly in front of you at the T-junction and the car park is sharp left.*

THE PUB
The **Fountain Inn and Boxer's Restaurant** will be found in St Thomas Street. It is a 16th-century pub with great character and is a favourite with the locals including the staff of the nearby Wells Cathedral School. Boxer's Restaurant has a Les Routiers menu and children are welcome (and have their own menu). There is an extensive range of choices on the menu including ploughman's, pasta, meat, fish, chicken and an exceptionally wide choice of tasty vegetarian dishes. From the usual snacks in the comfortable bar to a full three-course meal, the food is excellent.

Opening times: Monday to Saturday, 12 pm to 2.30 pm and 6 pm to 11 pm; Sunday 12 noon to 3 pm and 7 pm to 10.30 pm. Meals are served from 12 noon to 2 pm and 6 pm (7 pm on Sundays) to 10 pm (9.30 pm on Sundays). Dogs cannot be catered for, other than guide dogs.

☎ *01749 672317 or email eat@fountaininn.co.uk for a copy of the menu; website: www.thefountaininn.co.uk*

1 Leave the car park by turning left along the short **St Andrew's Street** and go straight ahead to pass under an arch. Just before the arch, glance right to see **Vicar's Close**, built by one of the bishops to enable him to keep an eye on his misbehaving vicars! Just after the arch you will enter into **Cathedral Green** with the magnificent **Wells Cathedral** to your left. Bear left to cross the green, keeping the cathedral to your left, and go straight ahead to pass into the market square, and then keep to the left to

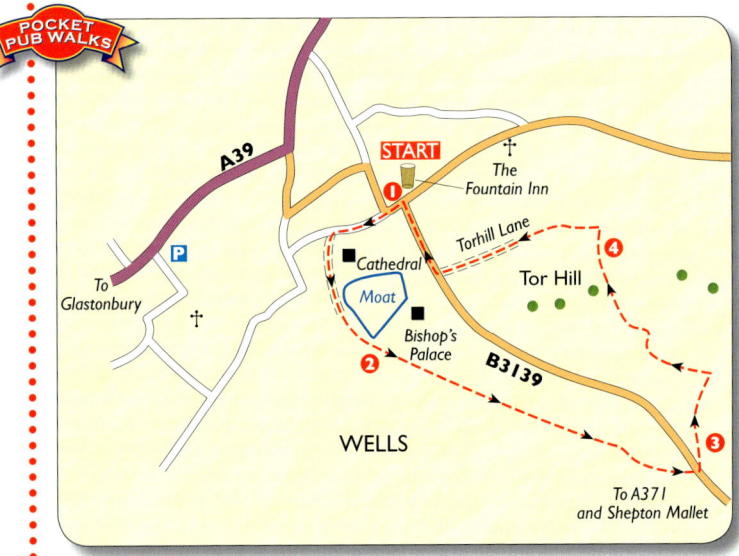

The moat at the Bishop's Palace, Wells.

pass under another arch into the grounds around the **Bishop's Palace**. Turn right to follow the moat around the palace, keeping the moat on your left.

2 Where the moat takes a sharp left turn, walk straight ahead, going past a 'Footpath to Dulcote' sign and through a kissing gate to follow a metalled path across the field, keeping to the left-hand field boundary. Continue along this obvious path, through another kissing gate, to eventually reach a road.

3 Cross the road and go through the kissing gate on the other side. Turn left, heading up a steep slope towards the **Pen Hill transmitter** and the top left corner of the field. Follow the left-hand field boundary until reaching a lane. Turn left onto the lane and almost immediately turn right to cross a stone stile marked as a footpath. Head left to the top corner of the field to enter a green lane. This curves right and then left before widening out into a field. Head for the waymarked stile in the opposite hedgerow to enter woodland. Go straight ahead into the wood, following the obvious path, to head steeply up through the trees. Leaving the woodland, cross a stile to head downhill towards a line of houses and reach a lane.

4 Turn left onto **Tor Furlong**, a significant track. Follow this all the way to the main road where you turn right onto **Tor Street**. As you walk into the city centre, you will see the **Fountain Inn** straight ahead of you.

Places of interest nearby

Wells Cathedral. The city of Wells takes its name from the holy springs, which are now in the centre of the grounds of the Bishop's Palace. The first church was built here in AD 705 and the cathedral as we see it today was commenced in 1180. Visitors are welcome and can join in a service or simply wander around. Admission is free although there are guidelines for donations since the cathedral receives no state aid.

The cathedral is open to the public from 7 am to 7 pm April to September; rest of the year 7 am to 6 pm. From midday to 1 pm there is a 'Quiet Hour', which visitors are asked to respect.

14 **Mells**

The Talbot Inn

The small village of Mells can boast historical and cultural links well in excess of its size. Here in the parish church is buried the war poet Siegfried Sassoon, and also Edward Lutyens, designer of the London Cenotaph, the magnificent Mells Park House and many other English country homes. The walk, which starts in this village, follows the peaceful, steep-sided and wooded valleys of Mells Stream on the outward journey and Fordbury Water through the wooded Whatley Bottom on the return leg.

THE PUB The **Talbot Inn** is a 15th-century coaching inn in the enchanting and historic village of Mells, strategically placed on the old London to Wells coaching route. It maintains the character and charm of a traditional village inn and can boast an award-winning restaurant with low oak beams and

Distance – 5 miles.

OS Explorer 142 Shepton Mallet & Mendip Hills East. GR 727492.
Mostly riverside walking on footpaths through deciduous woodland (be prepared for some mud after wet weather). Several stiles. Short section on a busy road just before point 7 of the route. Small ascents only.

Starting point Talbot Inn, Mells. The pub has a very small car park which is shared with the garage next door. Hence roadside parking is the best option and is only a problem if there is a wedding at the nearby church.

How to get there *From the A362 between Radstock and Frome, take the minor road south, signposted to Mells. On reaching the village centre at the bottom of the hill, turn right to go past the post office and the Talbot Inn is just after the parish church.*

a Tythe Barn bar. An à la carte menu of traditional English food features the best of the local produce. Sunday lunch here has been described as an institution – so be sure to book early if it's a Sunday lunch and walk that you're planning. Outside is a well-maintained garden and cobbled courtyard, which is really pleasant on a sunny day. Dogs on leads are welcome except in the restaurant.

Opening hours: 12 noon to 2 pm and 6 pm to 10.30 pm throughout the week. Food is served from 12 noon to 1.45 pm and 7 pm to 9 pm.
☎ *01373 812254; email: enquiries@talbotinn.com website: www.talbotinn.com*

1 Head east and downhill from the **Talbot Inn**, bearing right at the war memorial. At the post office, take the second turning left (not into **Park Hill**), signposted to **Great Elm** and **Frome**.

2 In 300 yards, turn right onto a bridleway and follow this along the deep-cleft wooded valley of **Mells Stream**, with the stream on your right-hand side. Follow the valley bottom for ¾ mile, passing steps, which lead up to your left, and the landscaped gardens of houses up on your left.

3 Turn right at a waymark sign and cross a grass clearing, sticking to the streamside track, to reach a footbridge. Cross the stream and turn left to follow the stream, now on your left-hand side. Walk beside the stream downhill for another 500 yards and cross a bridge over **Fordbury Water**, which joins the **Mells Stream** here.

4 Follow the track for a few yards and as you approach the road at **Great Elm**, turn right onto a track which goes through a gate

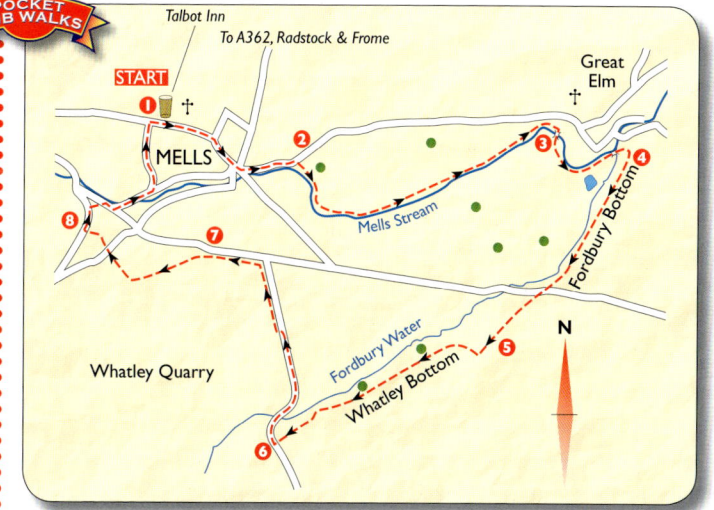

Mells Stream, which runs at the heart of the village.

into the woods. The path is not so distinct here but follow it uphill into the woods to reach a well-defined track. Turn right onto the track and follow it along **Fordbury Bottom** to reach a metalled road. Cross the road and continue in the same direction by going over a stile on the opposite side to follow a green track into a field. Walk alongside the left-hand field boundary to reach the far corner of the field.

5 Ignore the stile that leads straight ahead and instead turn right onto a track, which leads downhill towards the woods of **Whatley Bottom**. At the end of the track, enter a field on the left and follow the right-hand field boundary with the woods of **Fordbury Water** on your right. Follow the right-hand side of three fields, crossing stiles along the way, to reach a short lane down to the metalled road.

6 Turn right onto the road and follow this as it curves right, then left, going past the exit from **Whatley Quarry**, heading uphill to pass the higher entrance to the quarry. Shortly after this, leave the road by crossing a waymarked stile on your left to follow a track parallel to the road, with a steep tree-covered embankment to your left. The path eventually emerges from the trees and bears left, following the road and crossing grassland.

7 About 300 yards after the track bears left, turn left onto another track that leads away from the road, following the line of overhead cables towards a wood. Just before the woodland,

bear left to keep the woodland on your right-hand side, taking care not to follow the left-hand track which leads off along the edge of a quarry. Pass under another line of cables and turn right to head downhill through a gap in the trees. Continue downhill across a field to reach and cross a stile, which leads out onto a metalled road. Cross the stile immediately opposite into a field. Keep the same line of direction, hugging the field boundary to cross this and the next field, emerging onto a metalled road.

8 Turn right onto the road and in a short distance turn right onto a green track through the trees to reach another lane in a matter of 50 yards. Turn right onto the lane and then go left at the fork, crossing **Mells Stream**. Follow this road as it bears left at the next fork to reach a T-junction at **Mells**. Turn right to find the **Talbot Inn**.

Places of interest nearby

The **Radstock Mining Museum** is an award-winning attraction that reflects north Somerset's past involvement in coal mining. Towering slag heaps still provide the evidence of the abundance of mining in this area. The museum is based right in the centre of Radstock and is easily found, with the huge pit-head wheel indicating its site on Waterloo Road, and it's a great place for children, with plenty of hands-on opportunities. Apart from the expected collections of archaeological finds, coins, costumes and textiles, there are plenty of social history displays, with a Victorian classroom, Co-op shop, miner's cottage kitchen and a reconstruction of a section of coal mine. Open Tuesday to Friday, Sundays and Bank Holiday Mondays from 2 pm to 5 pm and Saturday from 11 am to 5 pm. Closed in December and January.
☎ 01761 437722; website: www.radstockmuseum.co.uk

15 Batcombe

The Three Horseshoes

Five miles south-east of Shepton Mallet**, Batcombe lies in the steep-sided valley of the River Alham and is well tucked away amidst deep combes and valleys. It is full of quaint cottages and the village itself makes a pleasant stroll for a quiet evening. This is a beautiful and unspoilt part of Somerset with quiet and narrow lanes connecting the scattered farmsteads. There are particularly fine views throughout most of the walk, which is a mixture of lanes, tracks and footpaths.

THE PUB The **Three Horseshoes** is a traditional village pub of 17th-century origin with open fires in winter and a warm welcome throughout the year. It is a free house and offers a wide selection of meals. Children are welcome and are provided with an adventure play area. There is a walled garden where

Distance – 3 miles.

OS Explorer 142 Shepton Mallet & Mendip Hills East. GR 689390.
Easy walking along well-maintained tracks with a little quiet road walking.

Starting point The Three Horseshoes, which is next to the church. Parking in the pub car park is very limited – please respect this and only use it whilst patronising the premises. Kerbside parking in the centre of Batcombe near the pub is possible.

How to get there From the A359 between Bruton and Frome, at Upton Noble take the minor road signposted west to Batcombe. Once in the village, follow the road through the village to a crossroads at the church. Turn right for the inn where the limited parking is for patrons only. Turn left at the T-junction beyond the inn, to park beside the road – with due consideration, of course, for the needs of the residents of the village.

drinks and meals can be taken and where there are sometimes summer barbecues.

Opening times: 12 noon to 3 pm and 6.30 pm to 11 pm (Sundays 7.30 pm to 10.30 pm). Food is served from midday to 2 pm and 7 pm to 9 pm, except on Sunday evenings when there is no food.
☎ *01749 850359*

1 As if you have just left the **Three Horseshoes**, turn right and then right again at the road junction. Follow the road for

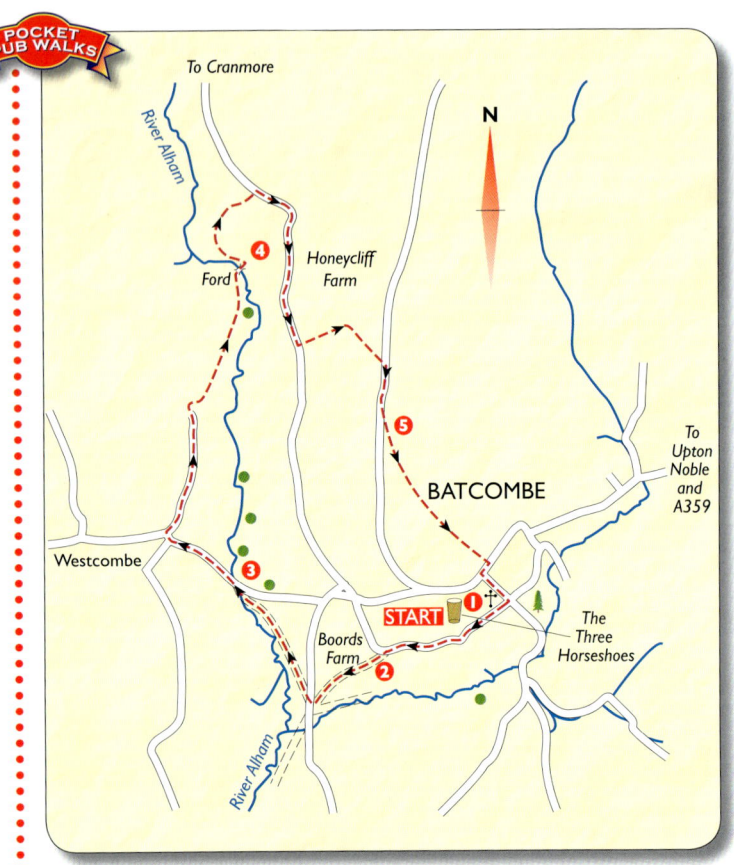

To Cranmore

River Alham

N

Honeycliff
Farm

④

Ford

⑤

To
Upton
Noble
and
A359

BATCOMBE

Westcombe

③

START ①

The
Three
Horseshoes

Boords
Farm

②

River Alham

POCKET
PUB WALKS

600 yards to a point where it swings round to the right at **Boord's Farm**, which will be on your left-hand side.

2 Just before the bend, turn left to pass through an alleyway at a cottage, beneath the archway displaying the date 1793. The path continues between narrow gardens to reach a stile. Cross this into the field and turn immediately to the right to follow the right-hand field boundary for a short distance and then bear left to follow the path as it slopes down across the field, heading for a gate which is just to the right of a bungalow. Cross the stile, onto the road, and go over the stile immediately opposite into a field. You will be faced with two footpaths, one that is signposted to the left (following your previous line of direction) and one heading to the right. Follow the one to the right as it drops down diagonally to the right, gradually moving closer to the stream on your left-hand side, which you follow upstream until reaching the metalled road.

3 Turn left onto the road and follow it into the hamlet of **Westcombe**, turning right at the phone box and war memorial, into the lane marked as a no through road. Continue for just over ½ mile to reach a ford. A little way before the ford, a stile on your left allows you to enter the field and follow the nearside edge to a footbridge.

Batcombe village.

Somerset

4 Cross the stream and continue your journey along the lane, past a farm, to reach a metalled road. Turn right onto the road and follow this until, about 200 yards after **Honeycliff Farm**, you turn left onto a track opposite a stone-built house on your right-hand side. Follow this track uphill as it doglegs to the right to reach another metalled road. Turn right onto the road, ignoring the signposted footpath to the left in about 50 yards.

5 In about 150 yards, turn left onto a stony track. Continue into the village centre at **Batcombe** with the **Three Horseshoes** just a few yards from the end of the track.

Places of interest nearby

The **East Somerset Railway** will be found at Cranmore station near Shepton Mallet, just 3 miles from Batcombe. Why not enjoy Sunday lunch or an evening meal on the *Mendip Belle*, a steam-hauled luxury experience through the Somerset countryside, reliving the nostalgia of the steam age. You may even be offered the chance to take the controls of the engine! There is ample parking for visitors, who can enjoy the Whistlestop Restaurant, which offers snacks and meals. The engine sheds and workshops are open to the public who can see how the rolling stock is maintained. There is also the famous **David Shepherd Gallery**, which features the work of this artist so well known for his paintings of steam trains and elephants, his two consuming passions. Trains run on Sundays from March to November, also Saturdays from April to October, and some Wednesdays and Thursdays in June to August, plus most bank holidays. The station opens at 10 am on days when trains are running. Closing times vary.
☎ 01749 880417; email: info@eastsomersetrailway.com; website: www.eastsomersetrailway.com